AF378273
WARS OF INDEPENDENCE 1286-1371
STUART 1371-1707
JACOBITE AND HANOVERIAN 1688-1746
AGE OF REVOLUTION 1700-1900
WAR + MODERN TIMES 1900-NOW

children's HISTORY of GLASGOW
Written by D. A. Nelson
CHILDHOOD DREAMS
HOMETOWN WORLD

How well do you know your town?

Have you ever wondered what it would have been like living in Glasgow when St Mungo arrived? What about rubbing shoulders with the finest people in the land in the Assembly Rooms? This book will uncover the important and exciting things that happened in your town.

Want to hear the other good bits? You will love this book! Some rather brainy folk have worked on it to make sure it's fun and informative. So what are you waiting for? Peel back the pages and be amazed at what happened in your town.

Timeline shows which period (dates and people) each spread is talking about

THE FACTS

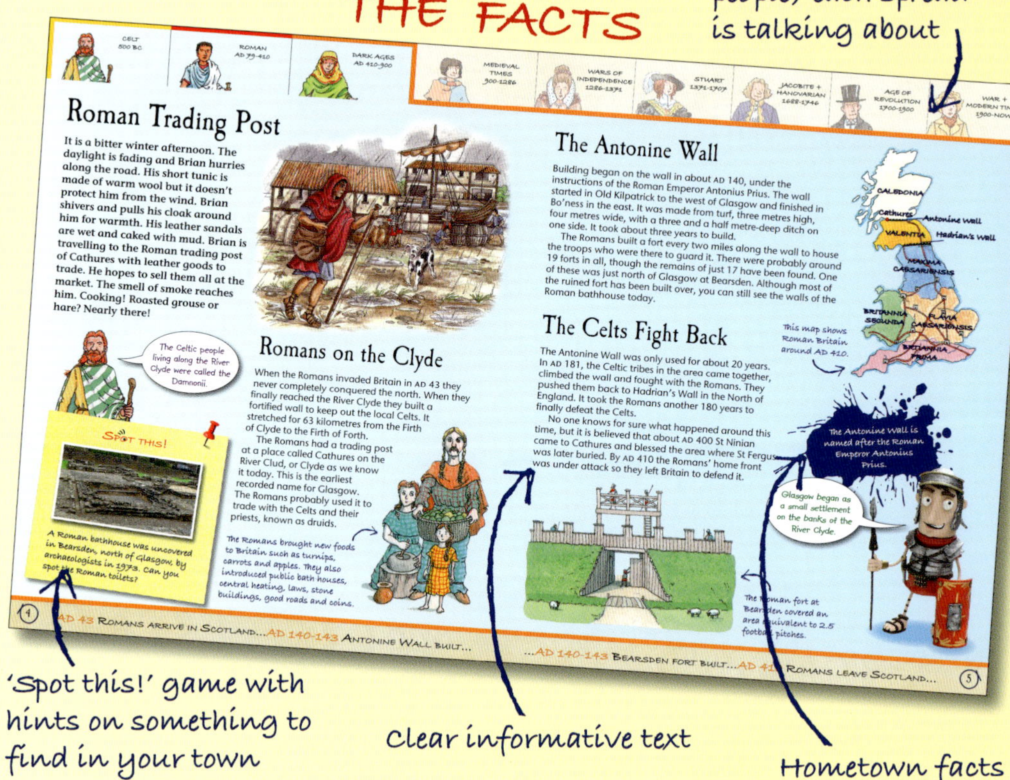

'Spot this!' game with hints on something to find in your town

Clear informative text

Hometown facts to amaze you!

THE EVIDENCE

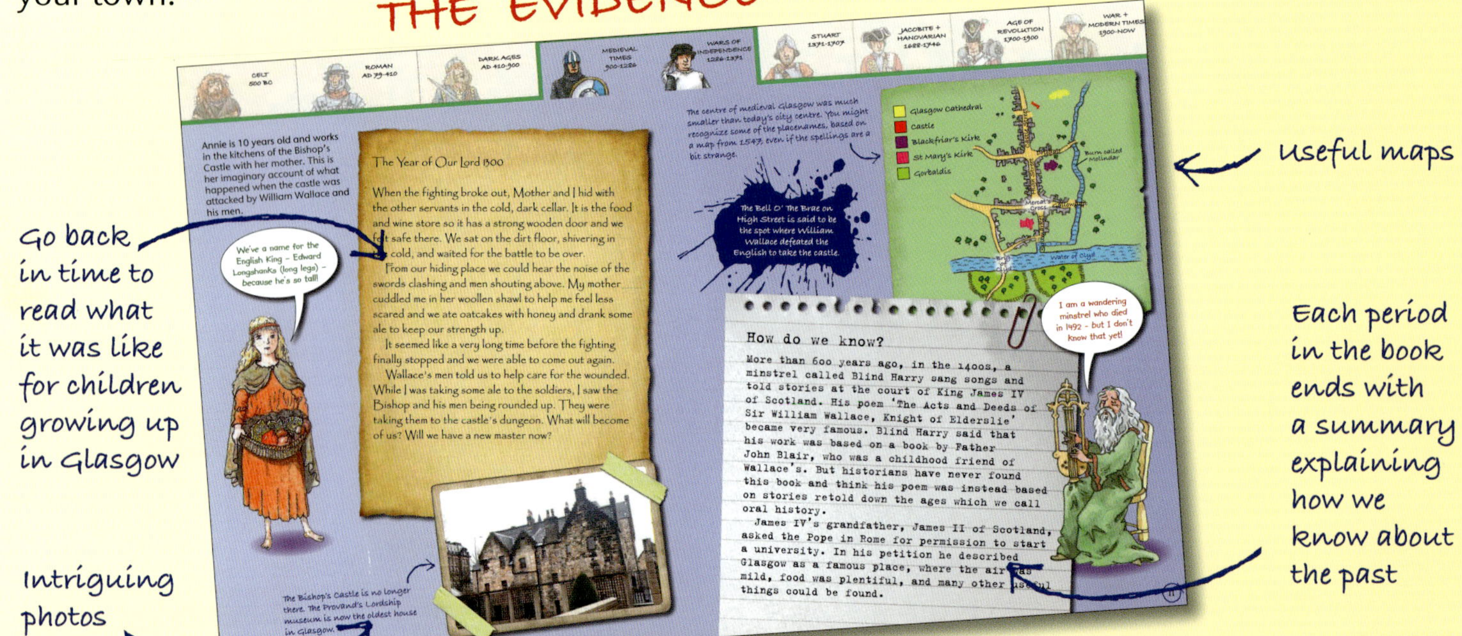

Go back in time to read what it was like for children growing up in Glasgow

Intriguing photos

Useful maps

Each period in the book ends with a summary explaining how we know about the past

Contents

Roman Trading Post — 4

A Holyman Arrives — 6

The Bishop's Castle — 8

Battle of Langside — 12

Bustling Quayside — 16

Clyde-built — 20

Glasgow at War — 24

Glasgow Today and Tomorrow — 28

Glossary — 30

Index — 31

Acknowledgements — 32

Roman Trading Post

It is a bitter winter afternoon. The daylight is fading and Brian hurries along the road. His short tunic is made of warm wool but it doesn't protect him from the wind. Brian shivers and pulls his cloak around him for warmth. His leather sandals are wet and caked with mud. Brian is travelling to the Roman trading post of Cathures with leather goods to trade. He hopes to sell them all at the market. The smell of smoke reaches him. Cooking! Roasted grouse or hare? Nearly there!

A Roman bathhouse was uncovered in Bearsden, north of Glasgow, by archaeologists in 1973. Can you spot the Roman toilets?

Romans on the Clyde

When the Romans invaded Britain in AD 43 they never completely conquered the north. When they finally reached the River Clyde they built a fortified wall – the Antonine Wall – to keep out the local Celts. It stretched for 63 kilometres from the Firth of Clyde to the Firth of Forth.

The Romans had a trading post at a place called Cathures on the River Clud, or Clyde as we know it today. This is the earliest recorded name for Glasgow. The Romans probably used it to trade with the Celts and their priests, known as druids.

The Romans brought new foods to Britain such as turnips, carrots and apples. They also introduced public bathhouses, central heating, laws, stone buildings, good roads and coins.

The Antonine Wall

Building began on the wall in about AD 140, under the instructions of the Roman Emperor Antonius Prius. The wall started in Old Kilpatrick to the west of Glasgow and finished in Bo'ness in the east. It was made from turf, three metres high, four metres wide, with a three and a half metre-deep ditch on one side. It took about three years to build.

The Romans built a fort every three kilometres along the wall to house the troops who were there to guard it. There were probably around 19 forts in all, though the remains of just 17 have been found. One of these was just north of Glasgow at Bearsden. Although most of the ruined fort has been built over, you can still see the walls of the Roman bathhouse today.

The Celts Fight Back

The Antonine Wall was used for only about 20 years. In AD 181, the Celtic tribes in the area came together, climbed the wall and fought with the Romans. They pushed them back to Hadrian's Wall in the north of England. It took the Romans another 180 years to finally defeat the Celts.

No one knows for sure what happened around this time, but it is believed that about AD 400 St Ninian came to Cathures and blessed the area where St Fergus was later buried. By AD 410 the Romans' home front was under attack so they left Britain to defend it.

This map shows Roman Britain around AD 410.

The Antonine Wall is named after the Roman Emperor Antonius Prius.

The Roman fort at Bearsden covered an area equivalent to 2.5 football pitches.

A Holyman Arrives

It is a beautiful spring day as Kenneth hurries to the nearby village of Glasgow. He's heard that the holyman Kentigern is there. It doesn't take long to find him as the village is small, only a few families. Kentigern is sitting on a rock outside the stone-built hut. Smoke curls from a hole in its peat roof. A small crowd has gathered to hear the holyman's story. Nearby a wooden chariot, pulled by two oxen, stands and lying inside is the body of a man.

Glasgow comes from the Gaelic for 'dear green place' or 'dear church'.

The Village of Glasgow

The holyman Kentigern travelled across Scotland from east to west around 1500 years ago. A legend tells of Kentigern following a chariot pulled by bulls that carried the dying Saint Fergus. This chariot stopped at a place we now know as Glasgow, on the banks of the River Clyde. When he arrived, there was a cemetery up the hill next to the Molendinar Burn, possibly started by Saint Ninian. Kentigern told the villagers of Glasgow that he was going to bury Saint Fergus there and start a new church to teach them about Christianity.

A Church

Saint Kentigern is better known as Saint Mungo – or 'dear one' in Gaelic. He is supposed to have performed four miracles. Saint Mungo built the first Christian church on the banks of the Molendinar Burn, in the area where Glasgow Cathedral now stands. Saint Mungo is thought to have lived for a very long time and died about the age of 85 – very, very old for the times.

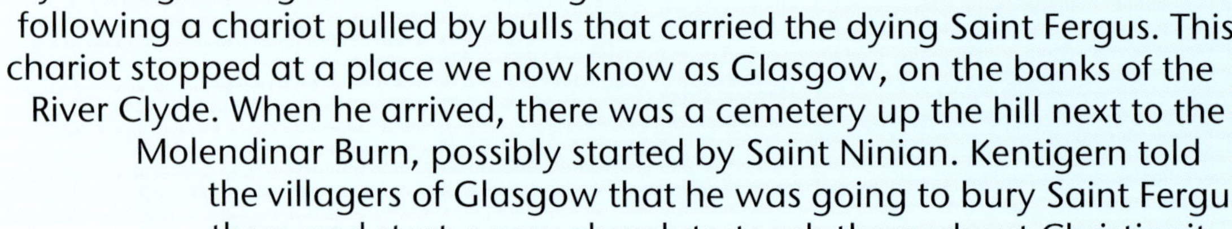

Strathclyde

Around the time that Kentigern arrived Glasgow was part of the Kingdom of Strathclyde. Strathclyde was ruled by the Britons from a stronghold at Dumbarton Rock for over 200 years. But, following a defeat by the Vikings, the kings of Strathclyde moved to Govan, the lowest crossing point of the River Clyde.

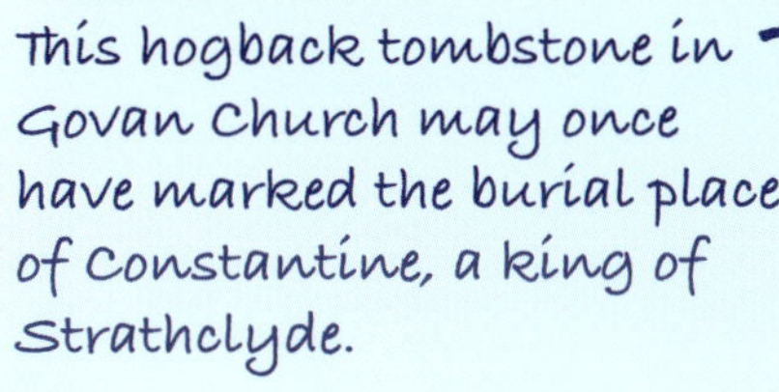

This hogback tombstone in Govan Church may once have marked the burial place of Constantine, a king of Strathclyde.

How do we know?

A lot of what we know about Saint Mungo comes from a book written around 600 years after he died. It was hand-written by a monk called Jocelin who lived at Furness Abbey in the north of England. Hardly anyone could read or write in those days but monasteries were places of learning. Many people believe that Jocelin had a book about Saint Mungo that was written in an ancient Celtic language. He translated the book into Latin, the language used in books at that time. Saint Mungo's four miracles are remembered in this popular rhyme:

Here is the bird that never flew;
Here is the tree that never grew;
Here is the bell that never rang;
Here is the fish that never swam.

Glasgow coat of arms shows Mungo's four miracles. Can you spot them? The rhyme on the right will help you.

You can see the tomb of Saint Mungo in Glasgow Cathedral.

The Bishop's Castle

Annie, the servant girl, puts down her pitcher of ale and runs up the steps of the castle. She works in the Bishop's Castle where the English Bishop of Durham lives, guarded by 1,000 English knights. Everyone who lives behind its stone walls is very nervous because they know there is going to be a battle. They have heard that the Scottish laird, William Wallace, and his men are marching from Ayr to win back the castle for the Scots. Now all they can do is wait, for they know the fight could start at any moment.

First War of Independence

It's AD 1297 and William Wallace, supported by 300 Scottish knights, is about to attack the Bishop's Castle to regain control for the Scottish people.

The English king, Edward I, had invaded Scotland the year before and replaced the troublesome Scottish bishop of Glasgow, Robert Wishart, with the English bishop of Durham. The Scottish lords and some Scottish bishops joined forces to fight the English. This was called the first Scottish War of Independence and it lasted for more than 30 years.

In 1300, William Wallace and his men attacked the Bishop's Castle and defeated the bishop of Durham. This meant that the Scots were in control of Glasgow once again.

This old engraving shows the Bishop's Castle in 1560 when it stood next to the Cathedral.

...1175 GLASGOW BECOMES A BURGH...1238 CATHEDRAL BUILDING BEGINS...

Wallace's Well

But William Wallace's victory didn't last long. In 1305, he was betrayed by a Scottish knight at a well near Robroyston. William Wallace was taken by the English to London where he was executed as a traitor. There is a monument to him at the spot where he was betrayed, called Wallace's Well.

In 1306, Robert the Bruce became King of Scotland, but the first War of Independence didn't end until 1328 when, finally, the Scots were in charge of their own country once more.

A Cathedral Town

By the time of Wallace's victory, the Church was very powerful. The town became a royal burgh in 1175 thanks to Bishop Jocelin. This gave merchants and local craftworkers, such as leather-workers, weavers and candlemakers, rights to trade in the weekly market. Some time before 1195, the church was damaged by fire. Bishop Jocelin rebuilt a magnificent cathedral. He also began the Glasgow Fair, which is still celebrated as a two-week holiday every July. The busy town's old wooden bridge was replaced with a new stone one in 1410. By 1451, Glasgow's bishop, William Turnbull, felt that the town was so important that it should have its own university.

A portrait of William Wallace.

The English king, Edward I, was known as 'The Hammer of the Scots' because of his brutal treatment of the Scottish people.

Glasgow Cathedral would have looked a lot like it does today.

Can you spot Wallace's Well in Robroyston? This is where Wallace drank his last drink before being captured by the English in 1305.

Annie is 10 years old and works in the kitchens of the Bishop's Castle with her mother. This is her imaginary account of what happened when the castle was attacked by William Wallace and his men.

The Year of Our Lord 1300

When the fighting broke out, Mother and I hid with the other servants in the cold, dark cellar. It is the food and wine store so it has a strong wooden door and we felt safe there. We sat on the dirt floor, shivering in the cold, and waited for the battle to be over.

From our hiding place we could hear the noise of the swords clashing and men shouting above. My mother cuddled me in her woollen shawl to help me feel less scared and we ate oatcakes with honey and drank some ale to keep our strength up.

It seemed like a very long time before the fighting finally stopped and we were able to come out again.

Wallace's men told us to help care for the wounded. While I was taking some ale to the soldiers, I saw the Bishop and his men being rounded up. They were taking them to the castle's dungeon. What will become of us? Will we have a new master now?

The Provand's Lordship is the oldest house in Glasgow. It is now a museum.

The centre of medieval Glasgow was much smaller than today's city centre. You might recognize some of the placenames, based on a map from 1547, even if the spellings are a bit strange.

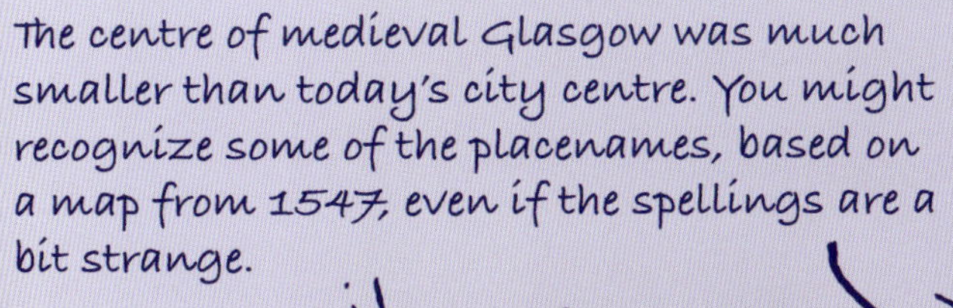

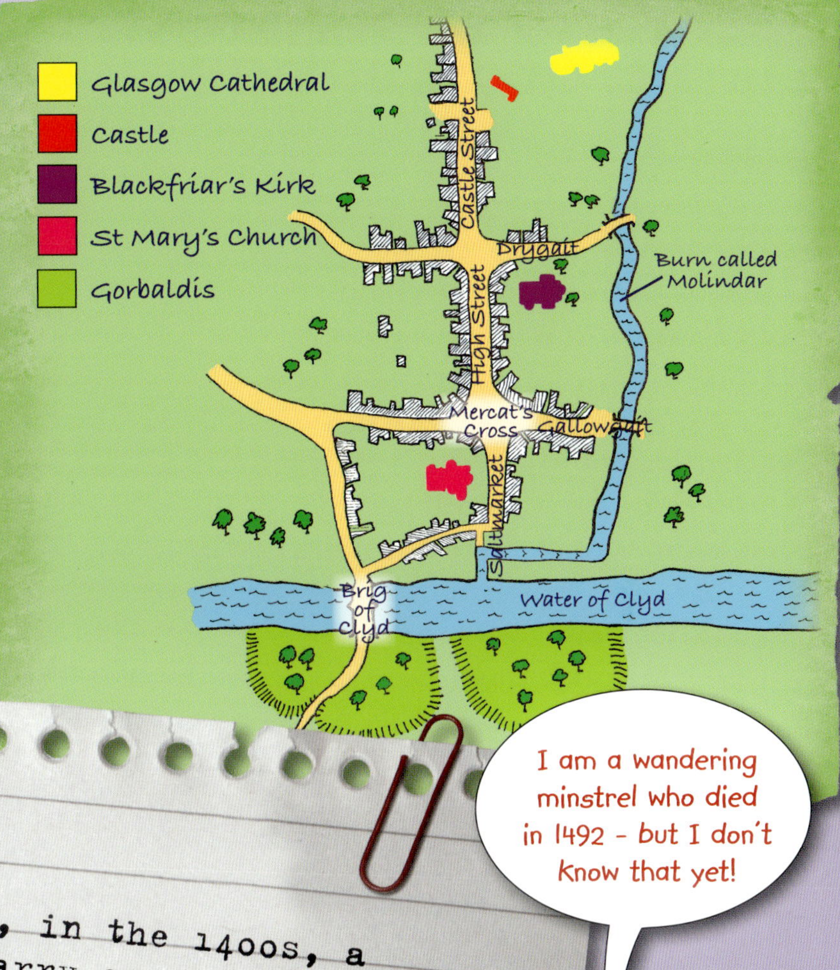

How do we know?

More than 600 years ago, in the 1400s, a minstrel called Blind Harry sang songs and told stories at the court of King James IV of Scotland. His poem 'The Acts and Deeds of Sir William Wallace, Knight of Elderslie' became very famous. Blind Harry said that his work was based on a book by Father John Blair, who was a childhood friend of Wallace. But historians have never found this book and think his poem was instead based on stories retold down the ages which we call oral history.

James II of Scotland, asked the Pope in Rome for permission to start a university. In his petition he described Glasgow as a famous place, where the air was mild, food was plentiful, and many other useful things could be found.

Battle of Langside

There is a rumble of cannon carriages, horses hooves and battle drums. It is 13th May, 1568 and Mary Stuart has arrived from Hamilton with her troops. She has escaped from prison and is trying to get to Dumbarton Castle. Regent Moray is trying to stop her and his men have been seen nearby. The villagers of Langside are packing up to leave. They don't want to be caught up in the fight.

This monument on Langside Hill marks where the Battle of Langside took place. It was put up in 1887 – 300 years after Mary was executed.

Royal Escape

Langside was a small village to the south of Glasgow when Mary Stuart (known as Mary Queen of Scots) and her 6,000 men arrived. Just over a week before, she had escaped from Loch Leven Castle where she had been imprisoned by Scottish lords who did not want her as their queen. She was making her way to Dumbarton Castle in the west to get help from her friend, Lord Fleming.

Unfortunately for Mary, she never made it. Instead, on reaching Langside, the queen found the way barred by Regent Moray and his army. A battle began that lasted less than an hour. Mary had many more men on her side, but Regent Moray's troops were better trained.

When Mary realized she was not going to win, she escaped to England to ask her cousin, Queen Elizabeth 1 of England, for help. But when she got there, Elizabeth sent her to prison. Mary was beheaded 20 years later because Elizabeth believed she was plotting to take over the English throne.

Merchant City

Glasgow was an important city by the 1600s. Scottish and European merchants who traded at the market brought their goods to the Tron to be weighed and measured. Then they paid tolls, or taxes, to the town's council at the Tolbooth.

Around 1600, Glasgow's Merchants Hall was built as a meeting place for the town's merchants and a place where merchants and their families who had fallen on hard times could go. The hall was rebuilt in the 1650s and had ground-floor lodgings for four old couples.

Tolbooth Steeple was used as a prison from where convicts could be transported abroad.

Tolbooth Steeple near Glasgow Cross was built in 1636.

Plague and Fire

Bubonic plague reached Glasgow in 1646. The town council sent the sick outside the city to Foul Moor and the city gates were closed to stop the disease spreading.

Another disaster struck in 1652 when a great fire swept through the city destroying a third of the town and leaving 1,000 people homeless.

The Tron Church Steeple at Trongate survived the Great Fire of Glasgow.

In 1557, Glasgow was only the 9th biggest town in Scotland. By 1670, only Edinburgh was bigger!

Port Glasgow

The River Clyde was too shallow for large ships, so goods were unloaded at Port Glasgow and taken up to the city on smaller boats. In 1667, Glasgow's town council paid for a new harbour to be built at Port Glasgow to help with trade.

James, a young boy from Langside, has returned to his village after the battle. Here is an imaginary account of what happened.

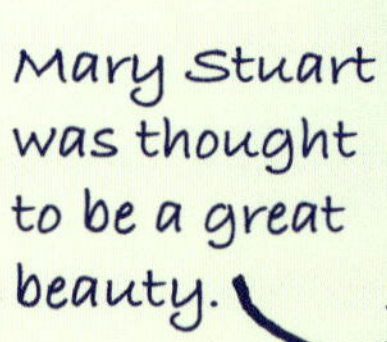

I have never seen so many soldiers gathered in the one place! There were thousands of them on the Queen's side, but not so many fighting for Regent Moray. We ran to hide in the woods with the other villagers, far away from the fighting. But when they weren't looking, I ran away and climbed a tree to see what was going on.

The air was filled with the smell of gunpowder and the sounds of cannons blasting, men shouting, horses charging and drums beating. When the smoke from the cannons cleared, I recognized the Queen right away. She was sitting on a horse some distance away from the fighting. Even from my hiding place, I could see that she was very tall, red-haired and pretty.

The fighting lasted less than an hour I'd say. As soon as the Queen saw she was losing, she and some men fled. Her followers also ran away, they scattered into the woods.

When the battle was over, the meadow was filled with injured and dying men crying out for help. Regent Moray's men rounded up any that could still walk. They will be imprisoned and executed as traitors.

My family is waiting in the woods. I need to tell them the fighting is over so we can return to our home. I thank the Lord that we have survived this ordeal.

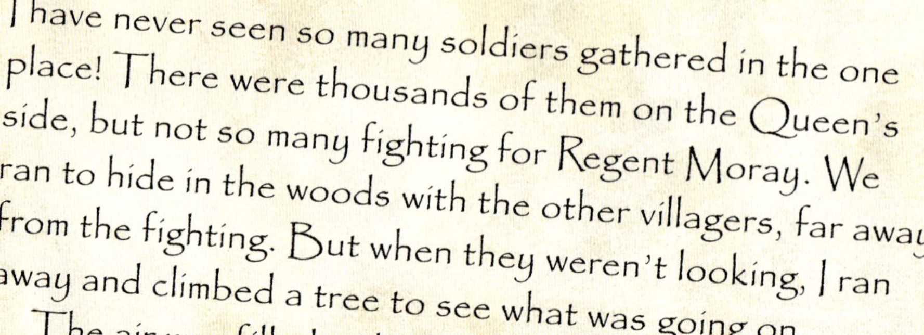

Mary Stuart was thought to be a great beauty.

This Queen Mary bawbie was found in a hoard of coins in Greenock. A bawbie was worth sixpence.

Dundrennan, May 15, 1568

To the high and mighty Prince, Elizabeth-

You are not ignorant, my dearest sister, of great part of my misfortunes, but these…have happened too recently yet to have reached your ears…I have since lost a battle, in which most of those who preserved their loyal integrity fell before my eyes. I am now forced out of my kingdom, and driven to such straits that, next to God, I have no hope but in your goodness. I beseech you therefore, my dearest sister, that I may be conducted to your presence, that I may acquaint you with all my affairs…

Your affectionate sister,

Mary

This is an extract from the letter Mary wrote to Elizabeth as she escaped from Scotland.

Hutchesons' Hospital in Trongate was built in 1639 to house orphan boys and elderly tradesmen. All that's left of it today are statues of the founders, Thomas (left) and George (right). You can spot them on the new Hutchesons' Hall.

How do we know?

There are a number of written accounts which have survived from the time of the Battle of Langside. Mary herself wrote a letter to Queen Elizabeth asking for help two days after the battle as she was fleeing to England.

Some of Glasgow's important charters were lost in the fire of 1652. But accounts of the fire survive. We know that within 10 years, Glasgow had its first fire engine and that candlemaking was banned in the city. The candlemakers set up just outside the city gates in a place that is still named after them – Candleriggs.

Bustling Quayside

Glasgow's Broomielaw Quay is bustling with ships unloading the cargoes of tobacco, sugar cane and raw cotton from transatlantic sailing ships that have docked downriver. The air reeks with the musty smell of dried tobacco leaves as porters heave the sacks onto their shoulders and take them down the gangplanks to the quay.

Tobacco Lords

In the mid-1700s, Glasgow was a busy trading city. Trade with the British colonies in America created lots of new jobs – everything from the sailors who sailed the trading ships to people who supplied the wealthy merchants with luxury goods.

The Tobacco Lords, or 'Virginia Dons', grew rich on trading with plantations in north America, including Virginia and the Caribbean. They were well known in Glasgow for wearing black silk suits, curled wigs, tricorn or three-cornered hats and bright red coats. They also carried gold- or silver-tipped walking canes.

The Tobacco Lords showed off their wealth by building huge houses for themselves and pavements that only they were allowed to walk on (everyone else had to walk in the muddy road). New roads were created and named after the plantations, such as Virginia Street and Jamaica Street. More bridges were built over the river. Glasgow was becoming a modern and fashionable city in which to live.

The wealthy tobacco lord William Cunninghame built himself a magnificent house in 1778. It is now the Gallery of Modern Art.

Plantation Trade

Glasgow was booming. The Tobacco Lords' ships brought tobacco, sugar cane and cotton from the American plantations. The ships docked at Greenock or Port Glasgow where the River Clyde was deep enough for tall ships. The cargo was then transferred into smaller ships and sailed upriver to the Broomielaw where the cargo was unloaded. By the early 1770s, the river was dredged of mud so that bigger ships could sail right into Glasgow itself. Trade associations were set up to ensure that traders supplying goods to the Tobacco Lords were fairly paid.

As the trade in cotton grew, so did the number of cotton mills that spun the cotton and wove the cloth. In 1787, there were only 19 cotton mills in Scotland; by 1834 there were more than 130 in the Glasgow area alone. The cotton mills began to export their cloth through Glasgow to America.

Tobacco ships unload at Port Glasgow in the 1760s.

Glasgow Green

In 1745, Bonnie Prince Charlie came to Glasgow. He was raising money and troops to fight for his Stuart claim to the English throne. He marched his army around Glasgow Green. But Glasgow's people weren't interested. They gave him 12,000 linen shirts, 600 cloth coats, shoes, tartan hose, blue bonnets and some money.

Another famous Scot came to Glasgow Green 20 years later. It was while James Watt was walking there that he thought of how to harness the power of steam to drive an engine.

In 1814, Glasgow Green became the first public park in Europe.

McLennan Arch on Glasgow Green was once part of the Assembly Rooms where the rich and famous of Glasgow spent their free time.

SPOT THIS!

Can you spot the James Watt boulder and the date 1765 on Glasgow Green?

Andrew is 10 years old and lives in a small flat in High Street in Glasgow. His mother died of cholera when he was six years old leaving 12 children for his father to care for. His father works as a porter on the Broomielaw, but he doesn't earn much money. So Andrew is going to be cabin boy on board *The Mary*, a trading ship bound for Virginia. This is an imaginary account.

1776

I can't wait to get out of this city and see the world. I've never been anywhere beyond Glasgow before. I hope to make my fortune one day in America.

The Mary is owned by one of the Virginia Dons, a rich merchant trading in tobacco and sugar to make rum. I've only seen him once, checking on a cargo we're sailing from the Broomielaw down to Port Glasgow where we'll load it on *The Mary*. He was a fine looking gentleman, make no mistake, right down to his high heeled shoes.

I have to go now. I'm being called by the First Mate of the ship. I'm finally leaving. My tummy is full of butterflies. I'm excited and frightened about sailing across the Atlantic. It's a dangerous journey, but worth it for the money. Just think, in 20 days, I'll set foot in the New World!

Tobacco was measured in 'hogsheads' – large wooden barrels that weighed about 500 kg full.

At the beginning of the 1700s, Glasgow was known for smuggling.

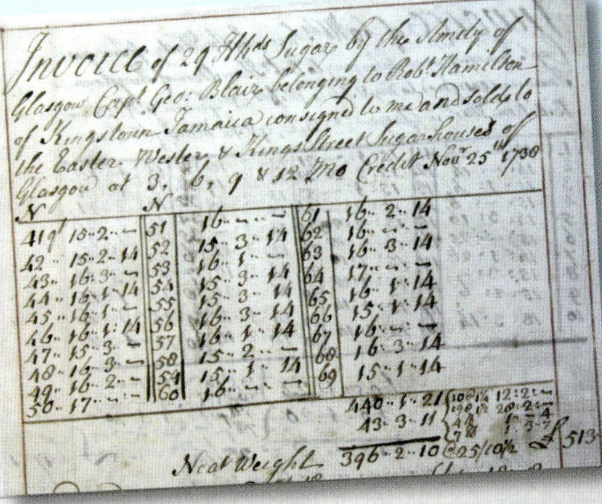

This invoice records how much sugar was brought back from Jamaica on the ship *Amity of Glasgow* in August 1730.

St Andrew's Church built by Tobacco Lords in 1756 - check out the ceiling inside!

How do we know?

The Tobacco Lords kept books or ledgers containing lists of the goods being taken out and brought back from America. Sailing across the Atlantic was a risky business. Cargoes were lost to bad weather, pirates or overloaded ships sinking. Insurance documents detail how much money a Tobacco Lord would receive if one of his ships sank during the journey to and from America.

Newspapers, such as the Glasgow Herald which was first printed in 1783, reported on the business lives of the Tobacco Lords, but also what they did in their spare time, such as attending balls and parties.

Daniel Defoe, who wrote 'Robinson Crusoe', visited the city in 1707, describing it as 'the cleanest and beautifullest, and best built city in Britain, London excepted'.

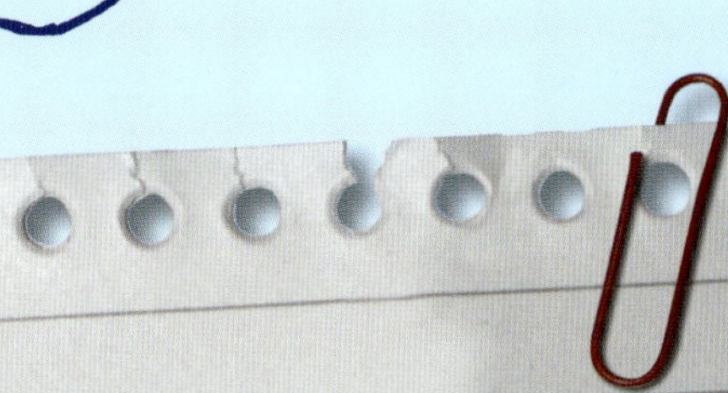

Merchant families built grand houses around George Square. The city council moved to Glasgow City Chambers in 1888 when it had grown too big for the Tolbooth.

Clyde-built

In shipyards up and down the River Clyde, men are busy building sailing ships and steamships that will cross the oceans to America, Australia, India and China. A heavy smell hangs in the air of hot metal, sawn wood and burning coal. The air is alive with clanging and shouting and the sounds of machinery at work, as slowly but surely they put together the latest magnificent ship to sail the seas.

Shipyards and Railways

If your ship was 'Clyde-built' it meant that it was modern, of the best quality and very reliable. Shipbuilders such as William Burrell, John Elder, John Brown and Sir George Burns designed and built some of the fastest and best ships the world had ever seen.

James Watt's new steam engine revolutionized shipbuilding. In 1812, Henry Bell's *Comet* steamed away from the Broomielaw Quay. The steam-driven paddle ship was an important invention because sailors no longer had to rely on the wind and tide.

The River Clyde itself changed. The river was dredged to make it deeper. More quays and docks were created on both sides of the river. Over 12 years the amount of goods brought into the city almost doubled.

When the new railways reached Glasgow in 1831 and 1842 they brought raw materials from the river to the factories and took finished goods from the factories back to the ships. Glasgow Central Station was opened in 1879. At this time Glasgow built a quarter of all locomotives in use anywhere in the world.

Passengers crowd onto steamboats at Broomielaw for a day out in 1876.

...1812 BELL'S COMET STEAMSHIP...1831 GLASGOW RAILWAY ARRIVES...

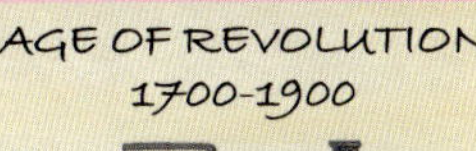

People and Industry

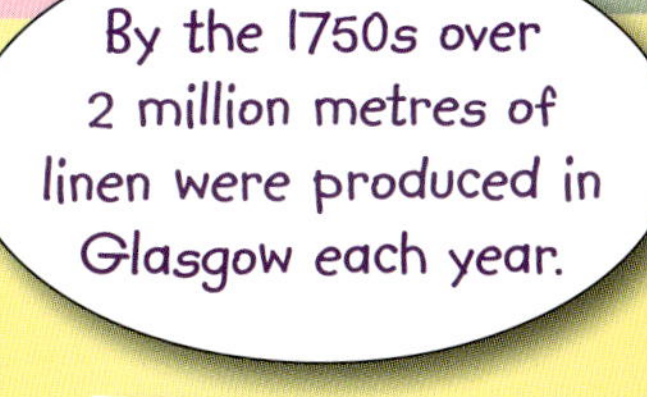

The shipyards created a lot of jobs for the people of Glasgow. Other businesses grew from supplying materials for the ships, such as timber, iron, sails, rope and other goods. Many people who couldn't find work elsewhere came to the shipyards to work. Glasgow's population grew enormously. Many of these were Irish weavers who found work in the mills.

One of Glasgow's best-known mills was Templeton's Carpet Factory. It was designed to look like a palace in Venice. While it was being built, part of a wall collapsed trapping more than 100 women weavers, and killing 29 others.

Templeton's Carpet Factory opened in 1892 and you can still see it next to the People's Palace on Glasgow Green.

Tenements

As the population boomed, the old tenement houses around High Street and Saltmarket became dirty and overcrowded. Diseases, such as typhus and cholera, spread. Joseph Lister, a surgeon at Glasgow Royal Infirmary, made the link between dirt and infection. He introduced antiseptics that killed germs and saved many lives.

The slum housing was cleared and new tenements were built in the West End of Glasgow. These were red stone buildings, 3–5 storeys high. Each floor was divided into 3 or 4 flats. People living in the building shared the main front door. Some had a tiled hallway and stairs known as 'wally closes'.

A photograph by Thomas Annan shows a family outside tenement buildings in Saltmarket in 1868.

SPOT THIS!

Can you spot St Enoch's subway? It opened on 14th December, 1896 as Glasgow Subway's head office.

Changing City

The city authorities and local businesses made other improvements such as new schools, parks, museums and libraries. John Elder, a Govan shipyard owner, provided education and an accident fund for his workers. The People's Palace and Winter Gardens at Glasgow Green opened in 1898. Kelvingrove Park, opened in 1852, took part in the great Victorian exhibitions.

George is 13 years old and goes to Govan Parish School. George's father is a draughtsman who works for Mr John Elder in the Fairfield Shipyard, Govan. His father's job is to help design sailing and steam ships for Mr Elder's company. George is studying hard as he hopes to become an apprentice to his father in the office.

Wednesday, 3rd June, 1862

After school, Mammy wrapped some sandwiches in wax paper for Father's tea. He's working late tonight. I ran all the way from Langlands Road to Govan Road where he works in the Fairfield Shipyard. I love to visit my father's office. I often go with him into the shipyards to see how the ships are being built. It's a dirty and smelly place, but it's wonderful to see a ship almost finished. The ship my father is working on just now is one that has a new type of steam engine in it, invented by Mr Elder himself. My father says that his job is very important because he is helping to create bigger, faster and better ships so that people can travel to far off places like America and China and Australia more quickly and safely. I can't wait to work there!

Glenlee Tall Ship was launched in 1896. You can still see it today at Glasgow Harbour.

The Clyde-built Cutty Sark was one of the fastest ships in the world and sailed between the UK and Australia.

Kelvingrove took part in the Glasgow International Exhibition of 1901.

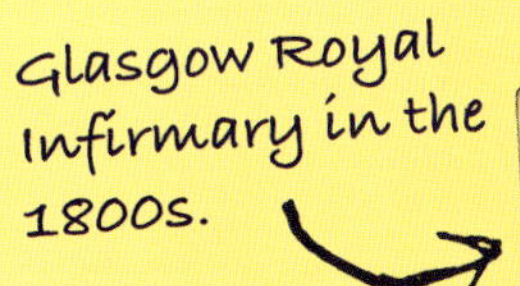
Glasgow Royal Infirmary in the 1800s.

The Earl of Roseberry opened the People's Palace and Winter Gardens in 1898.

How do we know?

Victorian shipbuilders and merchants kept records of their ships including their size, how much they cost to build, who they were built for, what cargo a ship carried and who sailed on them. They had paintings made of their ships and themselves. When photography became popular, they had photographs taken. Local newspapers printed stories about ships being launched and lost at sea.

James Watt recorded in his diary that his idea for using steam to drive an engine came to him as he was walking on Glasgow Green one Sunday:

"I had not walked further than the golf house when the whole thing was arranged in my mind."

Scotland Street School was designed by the famous Glasgow architect Charles Rennie Mackintosh and opened in 1906. Now it is a Museum of Education where you can find out what it was like to go to school in Victorian Glasgow.

The Tenement House in Garnethill has been kept just as it would have been in Victorian times. It still has a tiled wally close.

Glasgow at War

The air-raid sirens wail right across the city.
There is a complete blackout so that lights won't
alert enemy aircraft to the city. Glaswegians run
to their air-raid shelters to wait for the bombs to
drop. Families huddle in their garden Anderson
shelters, others hide in the Underground, yet
more run to municipal shelters across the city.
The thing they dreaded most has come true –
the German Luftwaffe bombers are searching
for Glasgow's weapons factories and shipyards.
As the drone of the bombers is heard overhead,
anti-aircraft guns along the River Clyde begin
firing. The noise is terrifying!

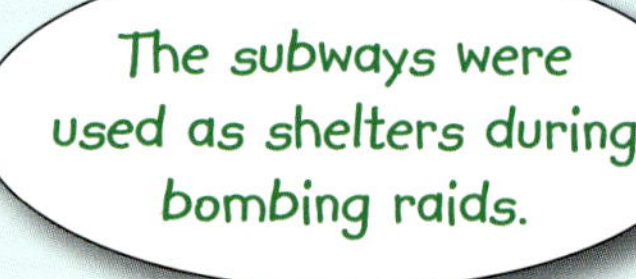

Blitz

On the night of 13th March, 1941, 235 German bombers
attacked Clydeside. Clydebank, a shipbuilding town downstream
from Glasgow, took the worst of it. Factories, shipyards and the
majority of houses in the town were bombed...many people
were killed, many more made homeless.

The following night, a beautiful moonlit night, 203 bombers
returned and this time it wasn't just Clydebank which was
targeted. Glasgow itself came under attack and bombs fell on
the city, including Maryhill in the north where there were army
barracks and the Rolls Royce factory in Hillington, just south of
the Clyde, which made engines for war planes.

In total, 1,000 bombs were dropped, 528 people died, 617
were seriously injured and many hundreds more had minor
injuries. Clydebank was totally destroyed and more than
35,000 people were made homeless.

Rest centres opened in schools and church halls to provide
food and shelter for people whose homes had been bombed.

Good Times and Bad...

By the 1900s, some areas of Glasgow had become overcrowded and run down. The workers went on strike to improve their rents, working hours and conditions. These protests, led by ordinary workers like Mary Barbour from Govan and John Maclean from Pollokshaws, became known as Red Clydeside.

After World War Two, Glasgow struggled to rebuild itself. In the 1960s the Cunard-White Star line ordered a new ocean-going liner, the *Queen Elizabeth II*, from the Upper Clyde Shipbuilders. The *QE2* was launched in September 1967 by the Queen. But many shipyards were forced to close, putting hundreds of Glasgow people out of work. The shipyards could no longer compete with cheaper industry abroad.

Two terrible tragedies rocked Glasgow. On 29th May, 1960, 19 firemen died trying to control a fire on Cheapside docks. A memorial statue stands outside Central Station. On 2nd January, 1971 a stairway collapsed at Ibrox Football Stadium, resulting in the deaths of 66 fans and injuring 200 others. A statue of John Greig, captain of Rangers at the time, commemorates the disaster.

The Gorbals in 1969. You can see derelict tenements.

The Gorbals today. Can you see the Guardian Angel?

On 27th May, 1927, John Logie Baird transmitted a television signal over 705 km from London to Glasgow.

...and Miles Better

In the 1980s and 1990s the Council and some other organizations came up with the 'Glasgow's Miles Better' campaign. They put on a Garden Festival in 1981; in 1990, Glasgow was the European City of Culture; and City of Architecture and Design in 1999. The same year, the national stadium at Hampden Park was rebuilt and the Scottish Football Museum opened in 2001.

SPOT THIS!

Can you spot the Finnieston Crane? It was built to lift heavy machinery on to ships, especially steam trains bound for other countries.

Agnes is 10 years old and lives in Maryhill in Glasgow with her mother and sister. Agnes's father is in the army fighting the Germans, but she doesn't know where because it's a secret and the government says: 'Careless Talk Costs Lives'. Agnes goes to school at St Mary's RC School on Kilmun Street. This is an imaginary account of the air raid.

14th March, 1941

We spent last night in the Anderson shelter at the back of the tenement flats. There was me, Joan and Mum with all our neighbours, so it was a bit of a squash. When the air-raid siren went off we were hoping it was a false alarm, but it wasn't.

At first all we heard was a whistling, then a thud, thud, thud as the bombs dropped. The whole place shook and my wee sister, Joan, started crying.

It seemed like ages before Mr Andrews, who is a warden, came in to tell us that the Germans were dropping landmines. He said there were two of them: one dropped on a tenement on Kilmun Street and the other on fields behind Duncruin Street. He says the school is badly damaged. My Aunty Liz and my cousins live near Kilmun Street and Mum was looking really worried. But we had to stay put until we got the 'All Clear'.

It was cold and dark in the shelter. We only had the one torch. Mrs McLeish, our neighbour from two up, passed around a flask of tea. It wasn't that hot, but it was sweet and better than nothing. Someone started a sing-song to keep our spirits up.

When the 'All Clear' finally sounded Mum went straight round to see Aunty Liz - they were all OK, but their home is wrecked. So they're all staying with us!

The munitions factory in Shieldhall produced the 'flying dustbin' - a tank mortar shell.

The Willow Tea Rooms were designed by Charles Rennie Mackintosh in 1904.

This picture of the John Brown shipyard workers playing football in 1967 shows the new QE2 half-built in the background.

How do we know?

A lot of evidence survives from World War Two because radio broadcasts and newsreels shown in cinemas still survive. Schools kept a logbook of events as they do today. Perhaps the most precious evidence we have is the memories of the people who lived through the war and who worked in the shipyards. Perhaps you have grandparents who remember those times. You'll find plenty of Charles Rennie Mackintosh's famous buildings all over the city, including the Willow Tea Rooms, Glasgow School of Art and Scotland Street School.

13-14 March, 1941
Air raid during night of 13-14 March. School in use ... as Rest Centre so classes did not meet. Kilmun Street suffered severely from explosion of land mine.

An entry from the school logbook for the day after the air raid tells us that the school was being used as a rescue centre for people whose homes had been bombed.

Glasgow Today and Tomorrow...

Glasgow's history can be discovered and enjoyed in lots of ways. You can see and touch objects at the Science Centre, visit Kelvingrove Museum and Art Gallery, walk through Glasgow Green and dine at The Willow. The important thing to remember is that Glasgow's history is about the people who lived through difficult or exciting or dangerous times – people like Brian, Kenneth, Annie, James, Andrew, George and Agnes!

The SECC & Clyde Auditorium is known locally as The Armadillo because of its shape. What do you think Charles Rennie Mackintosh would have made of it?

Glasgow is the largest city in Scotland!

The Glasgow Science Centre stands on the Clyde Waterfront where ships once unloaded cargo at Prince's Dock.

Fossil Grove, in Victoria Park, was uncovered in 1875. It is the fossilized remains of a forest that grew here over 300 million years ago when Glasgow was nearer the equator! You can visit Fossil Grove between April and September.

...2014 GLASGOW HOSTS COMMONWEALTH GAMES...

The Old Firm, Celtic and Rangers, have been playing each other since 1888. Will they still be rivals in 100 years?

Glasgow University can boast connections with many famous people, including Joseph Lister, John Logie Baird and James Watt. Can you spot the sign?

Celtic Park is the home of Celtic FC. It's the biggest football ground in Scotland.

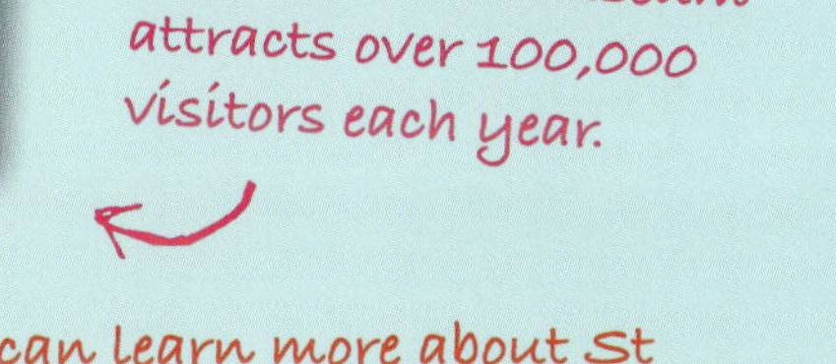

Hampden Park is the home of Rangers FC and the Scottish Football Museum. The museum attracts over 100,000 visitors each year.

The Clyde Arc, known as the Squinty Bridge, opened in 2008.

You can learn more about St Kentigern, the founder of Glasgow, at St Mungo's Museum of Religious Life and Art in Cathedral Square.

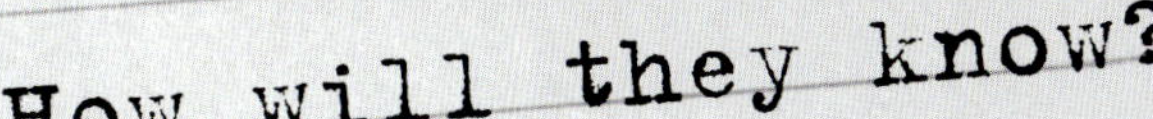

How will they know?

Will Glasgow always look like it does today? How will future generations know what the city was like today? The Internet is a great way of recording what Glasgow is like today. Photos, blogs and stories from tourists can all spread the word about our wonderful Glasgow. Or maybe you'll be famous one day and put Glasgow on the map!

Glossary

Abbey – a Christian monastery or convent, run by an abbott.

AD – a short way of writing the Latin words anno Domini, which mean 'in the year of our Lord', i.e. after the birth of Christ.

Anderson shelter – an air raid shelter used during World War Two, made from corrugated iron sheets and buried in people's gardens with earth piled on top.

Archaeologist – a person who studies the past by looking at the remains left by people in the past.

BC – a short way of writing 'before the birth of Christ'.

Blitz, the – when the Germans bombed towns during World War Two.

Burgh – an area, usually a town, with a charter which grants limited powers to govern itself.

Charter – a document giving certain authority or rights.

Coat of Arms – a design, usually including a shield, that has symbols representing a country, city, family or organization.

Fort – a large, strong building offering support and protection.

Gaelic – language of the Celts in Ireland and Scotland.

Kirk – a Scots word for church.

Latin – a language originally spoken in Ancient Rome.

Medieval – another term for the Middle Ages.

Merchant – a person who buys and sells goods in order to make a living.

Middle Ages – a period of time beginning roughly from AD 900 and overlapping with the Scottish Wars of Independence.

Minstrel – a medieval musician who sang songs which told stories about distant places or about real or imaginary historical events.

Monastery – a place where monks live and worship.

Monk – a male member of a religious community that has rules of poverty, chastity and obedience.

Pitcher – an open vessel with a handle and a spout for pouring.

Plague – a serious disease that is carried by rats and can be transferred to humans by fleas.

Quay – a wharf where ships can load and unload.

Regent – someone who rules during the absence of the country's king or queen.

Steeple – a tall tower that tapers to a point at the top.

Tenement – a building that is divided up into apartments or flats and is rented out.

Wally close – a tiled entrance to a tenement.

Index

Act of Union, 16
Antonine Wall, 4, 5

Baird, John Logie, 25, 29
Barbour, Mary, 25
Bearsden Fort, 4, 5
Bell, Henry, 20
Bell o'the Brae, 11
Bishop's Castle, 8, 9, 10, 11
Blind Harry, 11
Blitz, the, 24
Bo'ness, 5
Broomielaw Quay, 12, 16, 17, 18, 20
Bruce, Robert the, 9
Bubonic plague, 13

Candleriggs, 15
Celtic FC, 29
Celtic Park, 29
Clyde Arc, the, 29
Clydebank, 24
Comet, 20
Cutty Sark, 22

Dumbarton Castle, 12
Dumbarton Rock, 7

Elder, John, 21, 22

Finnieston Crane, 25
Firth of Clyde, 4
Firth of Forth, 4
Fossil Grove, 28

Gallery of Modern Art, 16
George Square, 19
Glasgow Cathedral, 6, 7, 8, 9, 11
Glasgow Central Station, 20
Glasgow City Chambers, 19
Glasgow Fair, 9

Glasgow, great fire of, 13, 15
Glasgow Green, 17, 21, 23, 28
Glasgow Herald, 19
Glasgow International Exhibition, 21, 23
Glasgow Royal Infirmary, 21, 23
Glasgow Science Centre, 28
Glasgow University, 9, 11, 13, 29
Gorbals, the, 25
Govan, 7, 21, 22
Govan Church, 7
Greenock, 16, 17

Hampden Park, 29
Hutcheson's Hall, 15

Ibrox Stadium disaster, 25

James IV, 11

James VI, 15

Kelvingrove Museum and Art Gallery, 28
Kelvingrove Park, 21
Kilmun Street, 26, 27

Langside, Battle of, 12, 14, 15
Lister, Joseph, 21, 29
Loch Leven Castle, 12

Maclean, John, 25
Mackintosh, Charles Rennie, 23, 27, 28
Mary Queen of Scots, 12, 14, 15
McLennan Arch, 17
Merchants Hall, 13
Molendinar Burn, 6
Moray, Regent, 12, 14

Museum of Education, 23
Museum of Transport, 22

Old Kilpatrick, 5

People's Palace, 21, 23
Port Glasgow, 13, 16, 17
Provand's Lordship Museum, 10

QE2, 24, 25, 27
railway, 20
Rangers FC, 29
Red Clydeside, 25
River Clyde, 4, 5, 6, 7, 11, 13, 17, 20, 24, 28
Robroyston, 9

St Andrew's Church, 19
St Enoch's Subway, 21
Saint Kentigern (Saint Mungo), 6, 7, 29
St Kentigern Church, 6
Scottish Football Museum, 25, 29
Scottish War of Independence, First, 8, 9
SECC & Clyde Auditorium, 28
Strathclyde, 7

Templeton's Carpet Factory, 21
tenements, 21, 23, 26
Tobacco Lords, 16, 17, 19
Tolbooth, 19
Tolbooth Steeple, 13
Tron Church Steeple, 13

Wallace, William, 8, 9, 10, 11
Watt, James, 17, 20, 23, 29
Winter Gardens, 21, 23
World War Two, 24, 26, 27

Acknowledgements

The publishers would like to thank the following people and organizations
for their permission to reproduce material on the following pages:

p4: www.catswhiskerstours.co.uk; p8: Glasgow Life/Glasgow Libraries (TGSA01014);
p9: Ben Allison/Flickr; p12: Photograph by Jim Campbell;
p13: kilnburn/Wikipedia; p14: McLean Museum and Art Gallery, Inverclyde Council;
p16: Finlay McWalter/Wikipedia; p17: Glasgow Life/Glasgow Libraries (Port Glasgow);
p19: jan 2004 05_RT8-Ayrshire Archives, reference DC 17-3; p20: Graham Lappin Collection;
p21: National Media Museum-SSPL; p23: Royal College of Physicians and Surgeons of Glasgow;
p24: Museum of the Order of St John; p25: Patrick Ward/Alamy;
p27: Trinity Mirror/Mirrorpix/Alamy; p28: www.RampantScotland.com; p29 Celticfcuk/Wikipedia

All other images copyright of Hometown World

Every effort has been made to trace and acknowledge the ownership of copyright.
If any rights have been omitted, the publishers offer to rectify this in any future editions.

Written by D. A. Nelson
Educational consultant: Neil Thompson
Local history consultant: Stephen Marritt
Designed by Jemma Cox

Illustrated by Leo Brown, Kate Davies, Dynamo Ltd, Virginia Gray, Tim Hutchinson,
Peter Kent, Nick Shewring and Tim Sutcliffe
Additional photographs by Alex Long

First published by HOMETOWN WORLD in 2011
Hometown World Ltd
7 Northumberland Buildings
Bath BA1 2JB

www.hometownworld.co.uk

Copyright © Hometown World Ltd 2011

ISBN 978-1-84993-191-5

All rights reserved
Printed in China

CELT
500 BC
ROMAN
AD 79-410
DARK AGES
AD 410-900
MEDIEVAL TIMES
900-1286